# ALL ABOARD READING™

Station Stop 3

# ICKSTORY

### An Icky, Sticky History of the World

## Unraveling the History of

# MUMMIES

### Around the World

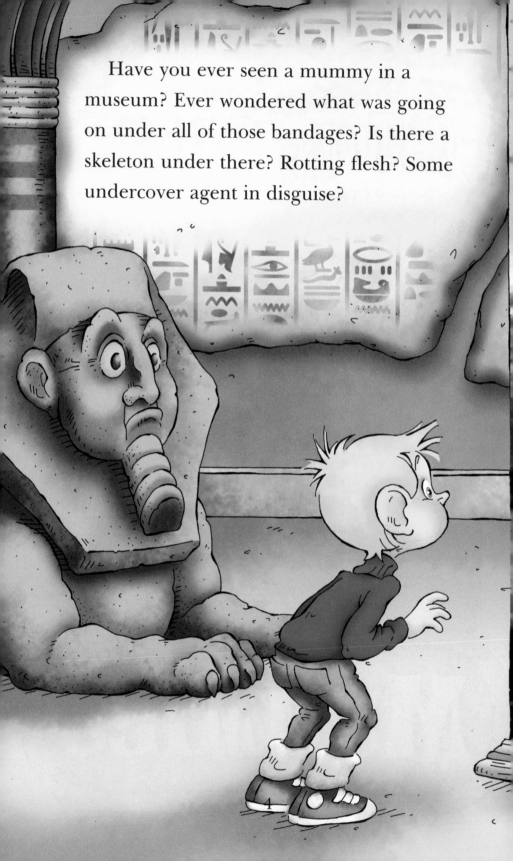

Have you ever seen a mummy in a museum? Ever wondered what was going on under all of those bandages? Is there a skeleton under there? Rotting flesh? Some undercover agent in disguise?

4

## Put Beginning Readers on the Right Track with
## ALL ABOARD READING™

The All Aboard Reading series is especially designed for beginning readers. Written by noted authors and illustrated in full color, these are books that children really want to read—books to excite their imagination, expand their interests, make them laugh, and support their feelings. With fiction and nonfiction stories that are high interest and curriculum-related, All Aboard Reading books offer something for every young reader. And with four different reading levels, the All Aboard Reading series lets you choose which books are most appropriate for your children and their growing abilities.

### Picture Readers
Picture Readers have super-simple texts, with many nouns appearing as rebus pictures. At the end of each book are 24 flash cards—on one side is a rebus picture; on the other side is the written-out word.

### Station Stop 1
Station Stop 1 books are best for children who have just begun to read. Simple words and big type make these early reading experiences more comfortable. Picture clues help children to figure out the words on the page. Lots of repetition throughout the text helps children to predict the next word or phrase—an essential step in developing word recognition.

### Station Stop 2
Station Stop 2 books are written specifically for children who are reading with help. Short sentences make it easier for early readers to understand what they are reading. Simple plots and simple dialogue help children with reading comprehension.

### Station Stop 3
Station Stop 3 books are perfect for children who are reading alone. With longer text and harder words, these books appeal to children who have mastered basic reading skills. More complex stories captivate children who are ready for more challenging books.

In addition to All Aboard Reading books, look for All Aboard Math Readers™ (fiction stories that teach math concepts children are learning in school); All Aboard Science Readers™ (nonfiction books that explore the most fascinating science topics in age-appropriate language); All Aboard Poetry Readers™ (funny, rhyming poems for readers of all levels); and All Aboard Mystery Readers™ (puzzling tales where children piece together evidence with the characters).

All Aboard for happy reading!

To my Mummy, Jean,
and my Mummy-in-law, Masako.—S.B.

GROSSET & DUNLAP
Published by the Penguin Group
Penguin Group (USA) Inc., 375 Hudson Street, New York, New York 10014, USA
Penguin Group (Canada), 90 Eglinton Avenue East, Suite 700, Toronto,
Ontario M4P 2Y3, Canada (a division of Pearson Penguin Canada Inc.)
Penguin Books Ltd., 80 Strand, London WC2R 0RL, England
Penguin Group Ireland, 25 St. Stephen's Green, Dublin 2, Ireland
(a division of Penguin Books Ltd.)
Penguin Group (Australia), 250 Camberwell Road, Camberwell, Victoria 3124,
Australia (a division of Pearson Australia Group Pty. Ltd.)
Penguin Books India Pvt. Ltd., 11 Community Centre, Panchsheel Park,
New Delhi—110 017, India
Penguin Group (NZ), 67 Apollo Drive, Rosedale, North Shore 0632, New Zealand
(a division of Pearson New Zealand Ltd.)
Penguin Books (South Africa) (Pty.) Ltd., 24 Sturdee Avenue,
Rosebank, Johannesburg 2196, South Africa

Penguin Books Ltd., Registered Offices:
80 Strand, London WC2R 0RL, England

Library of Congress Control Number: 2009017630

ISBN 978-0-448-45033-9                  10 9 8 7 6 5 4 3 2 1

Maybe you have seen movies where mummies awaken from the dead. Someone always shouts: "It's alive. Run!" Of course mummies can't really be woken from the dead. But they have other ways to tell their stories.

# CHAPTER I
## What Is A Mummy Anyway?

Any dead body that has been preserved is a mummy. After death, the flesh on most bodies rots and falls off. These bodies become skeletons—just a bunch of bones. But a dead body that has been preserved keeps its skin and flesh. This is what we call a mummy. Sometimes mummies are made on purpose: People use special methods to treat the body. Other times mummies are made by accident when nature exposes a dead body to extreme heat, cold, or chemicals.

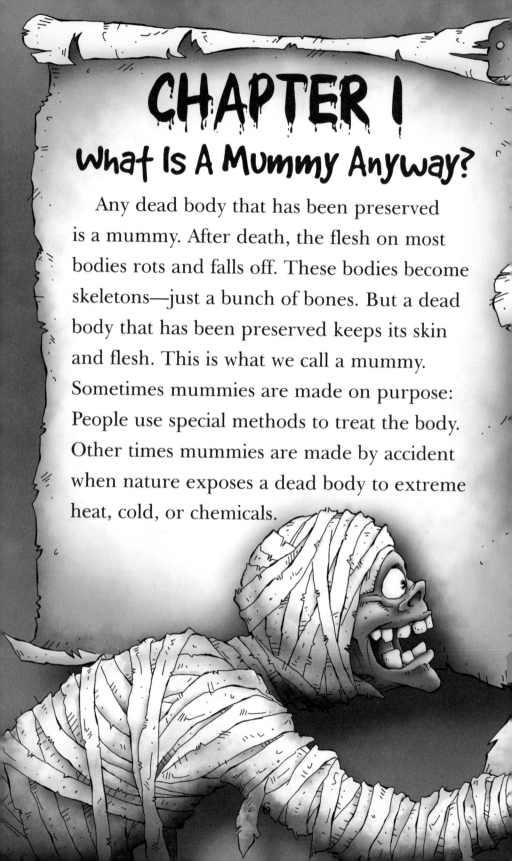

Mummified bodies of people and animals are found all over the world. Mummies are fascinating because not only are they preserved dead bodies, but they also teach us a lot about the way people lived a long time ago.

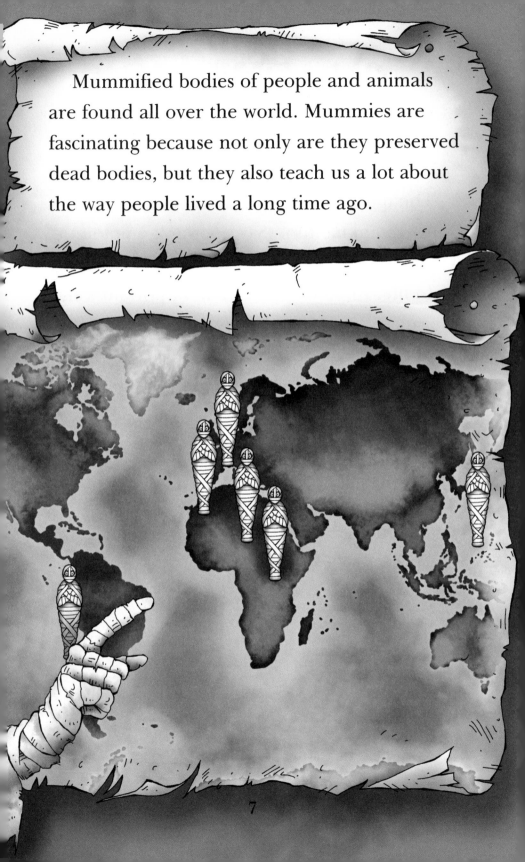

# CHAPTER 2
## Homemade Mummies

The most famous mummy is the Egyptian King Tutankhamun. (Say: toot-ank-ommon.) He died over 3,000 years ago.

In life, King Tut was not an important king. He ruled Egypt from the age of 8 until 19. It wasn't until 1922 that he became a household name. An archeologist opened his tomb. Besides Tut's body, there were chairs, games, and jewelry inside: Everything he would need in the afterlife.

How did the boy die? He was so young; people wondered if he was murdered. But scientists were able to look beneath the bandages and all the way down to his bones by using special scanning machines. The scientists discovered that King Tut actually died from a broken leg that became infected.

Special priests called embalmers took 70 days to turn Tut's body into a mummy. You could say those embalmers got all wrapped up!

First the embalmers removed all of his organs, except his heart. Egyptians believed the god of the underworld weighed a person's heart to determine if they would be allowed into the underworld.

Next, they removed King Tut's lungs, stomach, liver, and intestines and put them into special jars. Then one embalmer used his thumbs to pop out the king's eye. *Pop! Pop!* If you think that's gross, just wait until you hear how the embalmer removed the poor king's brains: He shoved a large hook up the king's nose and twirled it until Tut's brains turned into mush and drooled out of his nose. Makes you think twice about picking your nose—doesn't it?

The embalmer covered King Tut's body in a type of salt called natron. After about 40 days, his body was dried out like a prune.

Next, another embalmer rubbed oils and perfumes onto the king's shriveled body. Maybe he was giving Tut the spa treatment to make up for turning his brain into snot!

Then the embalmer used a plant sap called resin to make a hard coating over the king's entire body. Long strips of cloth were wrapped around his fingers, toes, arms, and legs. The embalmer slipped good luck charms between the strips as he wrapped the king. Finally, the whole body was wound in cloth.

As a finishing touch, a crown was placed on the mummy's head. A solid gold mask covered the king's face and shoulders. The king was now all dressed up and ready to go onto the next life. They tucked him inside a coffin, placed the coffin inside a large tomb, and plugged the openings with stone blocks. For over 3,000 years, King Tut was unknown. After the opening of his grave, the boy king became a mummy superstar.

The Chinchorros of South America were the first people to make mummies on purpose. Many of the mummies were children. Much like rag dolls, their bodies were stuffed with grass. You might even mistake a Chinchorro mummy for a doll!

Sometimes a wig was placed on the mummy's head. The Chinchorros liked their mummy dolls so much, they brought them home for a while before being buried. Those dolls might not have had much to say, but they sure were easy on the family's food bill!

When someone died in ancient Peru, the living arranged the body into the fetal position, wrapped it in layers of woven cloth, and put it into a sack. Then they decorated the outside of the sack, placed it in a tomb, and buried it along with the dead person's possessions. The more important the person, the more items were included. Thousands of mummy bundles were buried in the mountains of Peru.

One of these 1,600-year-old mummies was different from all the rest. Her body was tattooed with animals and patterns. Unusual items were found in her mummy bundle. She was probably someone important . . .

It turns out that she was a princess—her name was the Lady of Cao. Her bundle was so heavy, eight men had to lift it from the grave. Near the Lady of Cao's bundle lay the skeleton of a sacrificed woman. This woman would keep the Lady of Cao company in the afterlife. Let's hope she brought a few good jokes and some magic tricks along with her, because she and the Lady of Cao were going to be together for a long, long, time . . .

The Lady of Cao's bundle contained hundreds of items. Inside the layers of cloth surrounding her body were the possessions of a Moche princess: gold jewelry, headdresses, needles, and sewing tools. But her bundle also contained two war clubs and 23 spear throwers. Like a Boy Scout, that Lady of Cao sure was prepared!

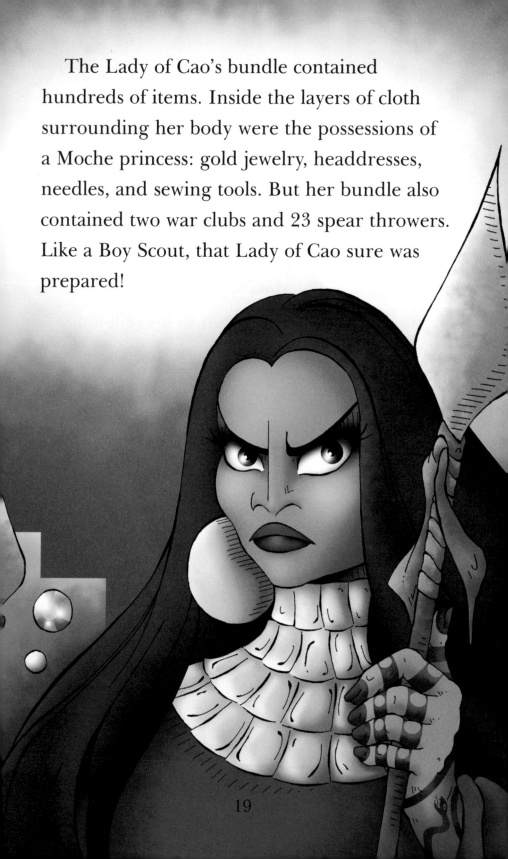

In the remote mountains of Japan are 19 self-made Buddhist priest mummies. One of these priests was named Tetsumonkai. (Say: tet-sue-monk-eye.) In the 1820s, he began the long process of turning himself into a mummy. Why would anyone choose to turn themselves into a mummy while they were still alive? Tetsumonkai, like the rest of those priests, wanted to show his devotion to his religion.

Tetsumonkai only ate nuts and seeds for 1,000 days. For the next 1,000 days, he ate small amounts of pine tree root and bark. These steps took away the fat and the fluid from his body. Also, he drank tea made from a poisonous tree. The sap from this tree tasted so disgusting that it made him vomit! But he drank it anyway because he knew it would keep bugs from feasting on his body after he died. Now that's devotion!

Finally, he locked himself in a stone room just big enough to sit in prayer. Fresh air entered the room through a tube. Each day he rang a bell. When the bell went silent, the tube was removed. The room stayed sealed for 1,000 days. When another monk came to open the room, he was greeted, or, er . . . not greeted by Tetsumonkai, the mummified monk!

# CHAPTER 3
## Accidental Mummies

The early Christians buried the dead in underground rock tunnels with compartments on the sides for graves. These tunnels are called catacombs. There are miles of catacombs in France and Italy which contain thousands of dead bodies. Most of the dead bodies are just bones. However, some of the bodies dried out and turned into mummies naturally.

In the late 1500s, monks living in Palermo, Italy, found mummies in their catacombs. When one of their own monks died, they laid him in the catacombs for eight months and then washed his body in vinegar. He became a mummy. When word got out, many local people wanted to turn their deceased family members into mummies, too.

In the fall of 1991, two hikers climbed up a mountain between Austria and Italy. They found a dead body sticking out of the ice. At first they thought this hiker may have died in an accident, but later discovered that they had actually uncovered a murder.

The police sent a medical examiner up the mountain. He determined that the body was very, very old: 5,300 years to be specific! The freezing cold conditions had kept the body from rotting. In other words, he was turned into a mummysicle!

The Ice Man was named Ötzi. (Say: utt-zee.) He is the oldest complete human body ever found.

An arrowhead in his left shoulder revealed that Ötzi was shot in the back. He was left to die on the cold mountain. Snow and ice covered up his murder for over 5,000 years.

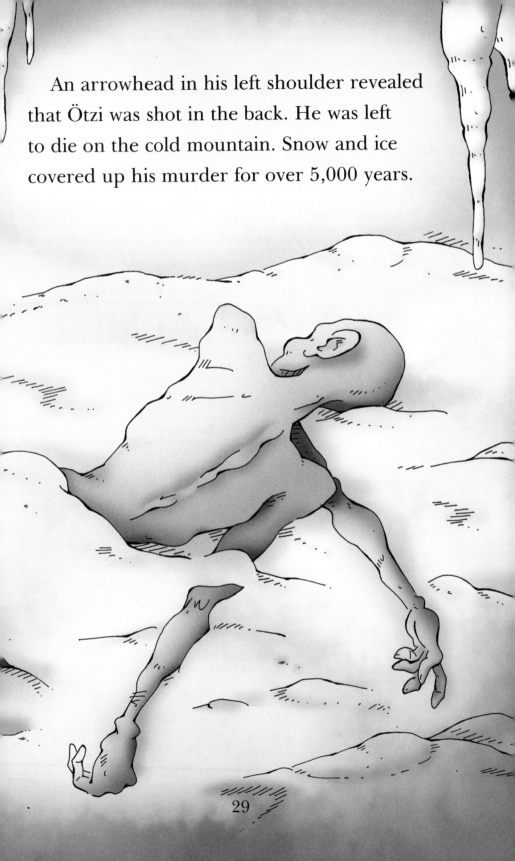

In Northern Europe, nearly 2,000 preserved bodies have been found in the murky waters of the bogs. Bogs are swamps where the chemicals in the water are perfect for making mummies. Some of the bodies were put there on purpose.

Many of the bog bodies give clues to their terrible deaths. Some of the bog bodies still have ropes tied to their necks, revealing that they were strangled or hung. Others have stab wounds or slit throats. The bog does a good job of saving the evidence.

When a body is left in the desert, insects or animals will usually eat it. But if the body is left alone, the dry desert air sucks all of the water out of the animal's body and turns it into a mummy.

The gravediggers of Guanajuato (Say: gwan-a-wat-oh), Mexico, had a big surprise in store for them one day in 1865. They were digging up the grave of a French doctor because he didn't have any family members to pay his grave tax. Inside, they found a mummified Dr. Leroy. The dry climate had preserved the body.

Within the next few years, over 100 bodies were dug up due to unpaid grave taxes. Can you guess what the town's people did with all the mummies?

They opened up a mummy museum! Each year thousands of people pay to visit these accidental mummies. Those poor souls made more money in death than they did in life!

# CHAPTER 4
## Mummy Fads

In Europe during the 1500s, people carried little pouches filled with ground up mummy. They used it as a lotion for bruises. Bloody nose? No problem, eat mummy powder.

People believed the medicine called *mumiyah* cured many illnesses. By the 1600s, doctors realized mummy medicine didn't really do anything, so the mummy powder craze ended. Aren't you glad you don't have to eat mumiyah?

The Egyptians mummified cats as well as humans. Cats were more than just house pets in ancient Egypt. They were worshipped. When a cat died, the pet was mummified and brought to the temple of Bastet, who was the goddess of women, children, and cats.

In 1888, a farmer accidentally uncovered a tomb containing thousands of cat mummies. He sold them for garden fertilizer! One company in England bought a 38,000-pound shipment that probably contained 180,000 mummified whole cats. It's a wonder cat flowers didn't start sprouting up all over the country!

Imagine using dead bodies as paint. From the 1600s until the 1920s, artists often used ground up mummies in their paintings. The pigment was called Egyptian brown or mummy brown.

One artist who used mummy brown paint in his paintings said a single mummy could make enough pigment to last for twenty years.

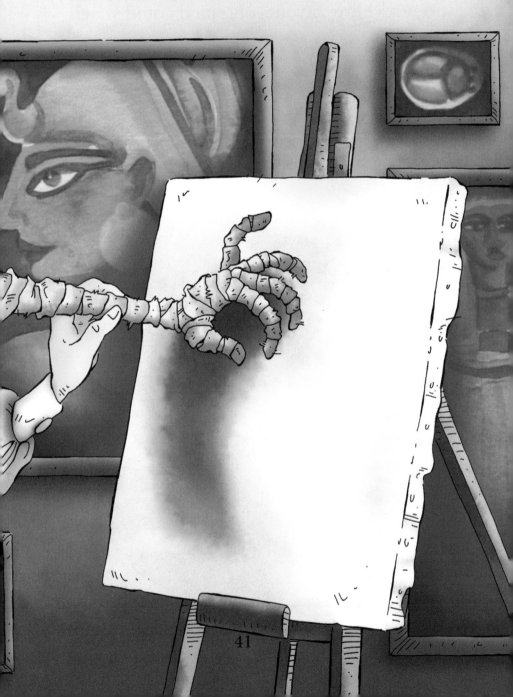

During the 1800s, unwrapping parties were all the rage in England. Some unwrapping parties were by invitation only. Others were big events where anyone who paid could watch.

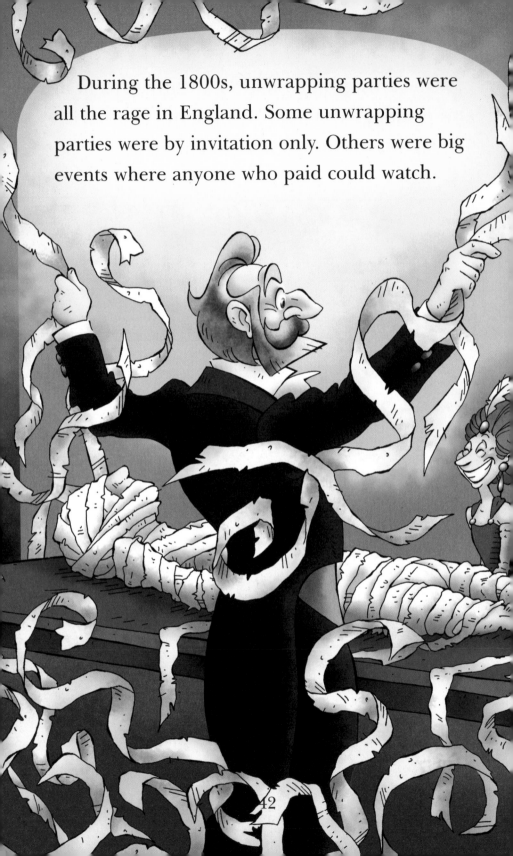

As each layer of bandages came off, the crowd's excitement grew. No one could wait to see what was underneath. Shriveled bodies— that's what! After everyone went home, the ancient mummy was thrown in the trash with the rest of the garbage. Imagine the look on a garbage collector's face when he found a body in one of the bags!

Some mummy collectors can actually be considered grave robbers. These robbers raided many tombs, but they weren't after the mummies.

They only cared about the treasures in the tombs and the charms that were wrapped in the mummy's bandages.

Museums collect mummies so visitors can study them and learn about the past.

Some people think displaying mummies anywhere is disrespectful to the dead. They think all mummies should be given a proper burial. What do you think?

Mummies show up in the strangest places. Bodies can be freeze-dried, salt-dried, air-dried, or chemically treated to make a mummy. The mummy can be an adult, a child, or even an animal. Mummies may not walk or talk, but they tell fascinating and unusual stories just the same.